SHIPS

THE FIRST RAFTS

Many thousands of years ago when the first primitive men and women lived, they did not know how to cross deep water.

Someone must have watched pieces of wood floating on the river. If the pieces of wood could float, perhaps a man sitting on a log would be able to float too.

In time, prehistoric man thought of tying one log to another to make a raft.

More than one person could be carried on a raft, and prehistoric man was on his way to inventing the first boat.

Dug-out canoe

Coracle

Quffa

Birch-bark canoe

EARLY BOATS

The kinds of boats built by early man depended on where he lived and what materials were available for him to use.

If he lived on the edge of a forest he could hollow out a tree trunk to make a canoe, or he could build a raft.

If he lived near a desert, his boats would be made from inflated animal skins. In swampy areas, boats would be made from bundles of reeds.

Eventually, men learnt how to make canoes from frames of wood or bone over which they stretched skins or tree bark.

Wood and bark and animal hides were all used to keep the first sailors afloat.

Many of these ancient types of boats are still used in many parts of the world.

Fishermen in India, Africa and Shrilanka still use log and reed rafts.

Dug-out canoes can be seen in Indonesia, South America, Africa and Australia.

Coracles, made from skins stretched over a wooden frame, are still used in South Wales and Ireland.

Viking long-boat

Roman galley

OARS AND PADDLES

In time, men discovered that a flat piece of wood or a
pole in shallow water, was a more efficient way to
push themselves through the water than paddling
with their hands. These pieces of wood were adapted
later into **oars** and **paddles**.

The first big ships used teams of oarsmen. It was
important that each man rowed in time with the next.
The Romans made slaves row their galleys. A
drummer beat the time. In a modern rowing race, the
cox calls out the time.

3

BOAT BUILDING

For thousands of years wood was the only suitable material for building a large ship. The type of ship that could be built and the length of time it lasted, depended on the type of wood available.

As men became cleverer with their hands and tools, they built boats and ships piece by piece, plank by plank. They built different kinds of ships with different shapes to improve the way they floated and the way they sailed.

4

Egyptian warship   **King Rameses III**

TRADING AND EXPLORING

As ships made travelling over water possible, it was soon seen that they could carry goods to trade with other people. They could also carry men to explore, to find new lands and new wealth.

They could carry men to fight and plunder, and bring back the stolen riches of other lands.

This warship had a battering ram covered in metal.

It was built to fight invaders from the Mediterranean in about 1200 B.C.

SAILING SHIPS

Men discovered quite early on, that if they hung pieces of skin or cloth on poles, these **sails** would catch the force of the wind, and the wind would push the ship forward.

The sails could be let down or **unfurled** when the wind blew.

If the wind was too strong or the ship did not move, the sails could be rolled up or **furled**.

The sail was hung from a bar of wood called a **yard arm** which was mounted on a pole or **mast**.

A system of ropes and pulleys called **rigging** was developed to control the sails.

Yard arm

Rigging

Mast

Sail

If there was not enough wind a boat could still move forwards because oars were carried as well as sails.

By the 15th century, as ships became bigger, more and bigger sails were used.

The ships began to have more than one **mast**, each with its own sails. Now better use could be made of the wind. Control by catching every puff of wind that was blowing, came from the **size**, **number** and **angle** of the sails. If the wind was too strong, some of the sails could be furled.

There still could be times when the wind did not blow at all. As the ships were too big and clumsy for oars to be used, the sailors could do nothing but wait anxiously for the wind to come. Every extra day at sea meant that their precious food and water was being used up. No wonder sailors were afraid of being **becalmed**.

STEERING THE SHIP

Over the years, a **rudder** had been developed to steer a ship. This rudder was like a huge oar, and was placed in the middle of the **stern** (the back of the ship). As sailing ships grew in size, a **tiller**, or handle, was attached to the rudder to control it more easily.

Stern

Tiller

Rudder

Sails became more important as men set off to explore the world. In the 15th and 16th centuries, ships captained by men who are now famous, Columbus, Vasco da Gama, and Magellan, sailed to discover new routes to India and the Americas. They brought home wealth, established trade routes and found unknown lands.

There was much competition between countries for the wealth of these newly found lands. For example, England and Spain were bitter enemies, and there were many sea battles between Spanish and English ships.

In 1577, Sir Francis Drake set out from England to sail around the world.

His ship was named the **Pelican** but he robbed the Spaniards of so much treasure that he renamed her the **Golden Hind**.

Golden Hind 16th century galleon

The **chebeck** was used by the pirates who plagued the Mediterranean sea in the 17th century.

It was very light, narrow and swift.

TRADING SHIPS

Countries developed settlements of their people called **colonies** in their share of the new territories. Trade increased greatly as the colonies grew and began to trade with each other and their mother countries.

Greater trade brought the need for new vessels to carry larger cargoes, and so ship design began to change again. Wide, deep, heavy ships were built to carry large amounts of cargo. Swift, narrow ships with large sails for speed were used for smuggling, piracy and trades where perishable goods were shipped.

By the 18th century the French and Spanish were building their own chebecks to fight back on even terms.

Chebecks had three masts and **lateen** or triangular sails.

9

**France
1911**

The largest
sailing ship
ever built was a
French barge
named **France**.
She was
launched at
Bordeaux in
1911.

This ship had
five masts,
weighed over
5600 tons and
was more than
125 metres
long!

COMPETITION AMONG SHIPS

At first the colonies were tied to tight trade
regulations made by their mother countries which
restricted their freedom of trade, but by the nineteenth century many of the older colonies had won
their independence and could trade with whom they
pleased.

Competition became very much fiercer. Each country
tried to build bigger and better ships to carry more
goods faster than their rivals.

Cutty Sark 1869

The greatest clipper races were on the tea route from China to London.

The **Taeping** and **Ariel** completed the journey in 99 days, and finished the race within a few hours of each other.

In the early nineteenth century, American shipyards began to build **clipper** ships. These long ships could hold a huge amount of cargo or passengers, and their swift lines, large sails and great length made them the fastest sailing ships of their kind. British clippers were built to compete with them, and there were many races over the trade routes between rival trading companies.

However fast these sailing ships were, they were still dependent on three unreliable forces of power to make them move—the force of the wind; tides and water currents; and the strength of human muscles.

The **Cutty Sark** was a British clipper, and was specially built to race a rival ship, **Thermopylae**, on the tea route from China.

This clipper was built in 1869 as a **composite** ship made of wooden planks on an iron frame.

11

British Queen
1839

STEAMSHIPS

For most of the nineteenth century, steam ships kept their sails in case of an engine break down.

The steam engine, invented in 1764 by James Watt, soon replaced the unreliable wind power. At first ships kept their sails in case the engine broke down, but once it was seen how reliable and powerful the steam engine could be, designers began to leave out the sails.

The **British Queen** was the first ship to cross the Atlantic entirely under steam in 1839.

THE PADDLE STEAMER

The first steamships were driven by many **paddles** fixed to a wheel. As the wheel turned, the paddles pushed strongly against the water and forced the ship forward. This motion was strangely like the paddling of the first boatmen in their canoes. Ships driven by paddles were called **paddle steamers**.

Paddle steamers were built in many shapes and sizes in the nineteenth century. Some were specially designed for the sea or coastal shipping, others for travel on long, wide rivers such as the Rhine in Germany and the Mississippi in America.

Paddle steamers on the Mississippi river were long and low with many decks. They were decorated with carved pillars and balconies.

River paddle steamers did not need sails.

These paddle steamers were like floating hotels. They had bedrooms, restaurants, even theatres and gaming rooms.

River paddle steamers are still in use today.

Mississippi paddle steamer

The Rattler

Foremast

Mainmast

Sails and rigging

Funnel

Mizzen mast

Lifeboat

Bow

Stern

Bowsprit

Hull

In 1845 the propeller driven **Rattler** won a tug of war with the **Alecto** paddle steamer.

Propeller's are also known as **screws**. This describes their movement through water.

Propeller

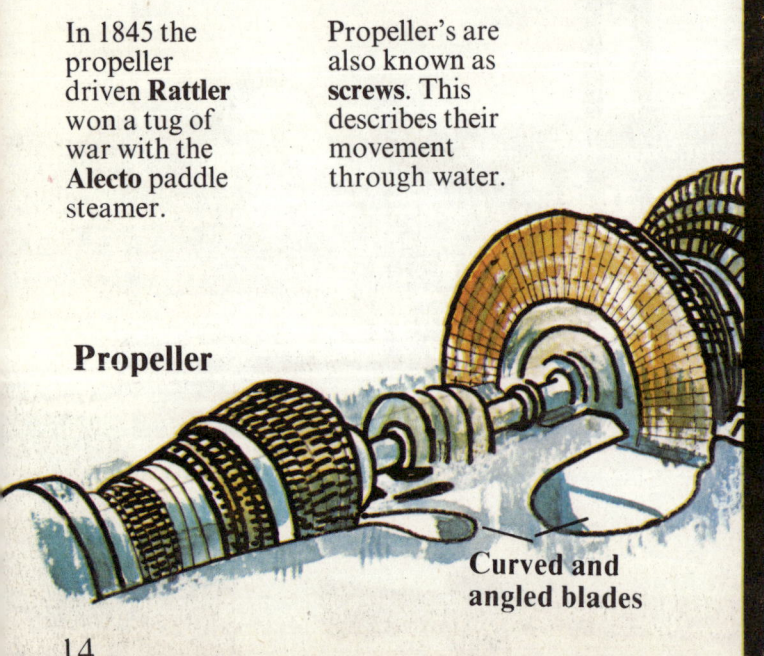

Curved and angled blades

THE PROPELLER

By the middle of the nineteenth century, a new invention, the **propeller**, began to replace the paddle.

The propeller's angled and curved blades pushed strongly against the water as they spun. This gave greater thrust than the straight paddle blade, and made better use of the engine power.

MODERN SHIPS' ENGINES

Nowadays ships' engines can be driven by steam turbines, diesel motors or even by aeroplane engines or engines driven by nuclear power.

A **Hovercraft** is driven by aeroplane engines. It moves above the water on a cushion of air.

The Hovercraft is one of the latest developments in modern shipping.

The Hovercraft can also travel over land.

Hovercraft

Captain's 'flight deck'

'Aeroplane' engines

Passenger cabin

Hold for cars and cargo

Rubber 'cushion' filled with air

SUBMARINES

The story of ships goes under the sea as well as on the surface. Submarines are the ships of this underwater world.

A submarine has a double **casing** or hull that can hold air or water. To move about under water the submarine's **ballast tanks** take in water until it becomes the same weight as the water around it. The submarine can be man-oeuvred up and down under water by using its **hydroplanes** which are rather like short wings.

To bring the submarine to the surface to move around on top of the water, the ballast tanks are emptied to make the submarine rise as it becomes lighter.

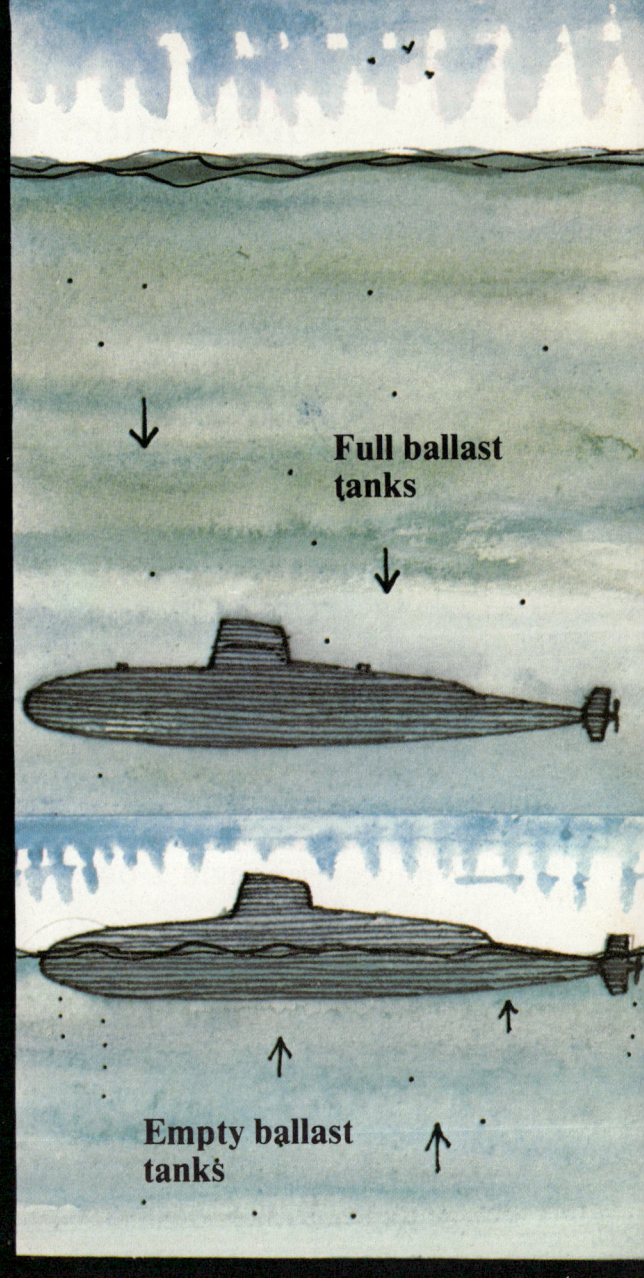

Full ballast tanks

Empty ballast tanks

Submarines are war vessels able to hide under water and attack targets without being seen. They fire torpedoes to sink enemy shipping.

The first submarine used in war was the **Turtle** in 1776. It was very primitive and a total failure!

16

Many submarines can now fire guided missiles with nuclear warheads from under the water which can reach targets thousands of kilometres away.

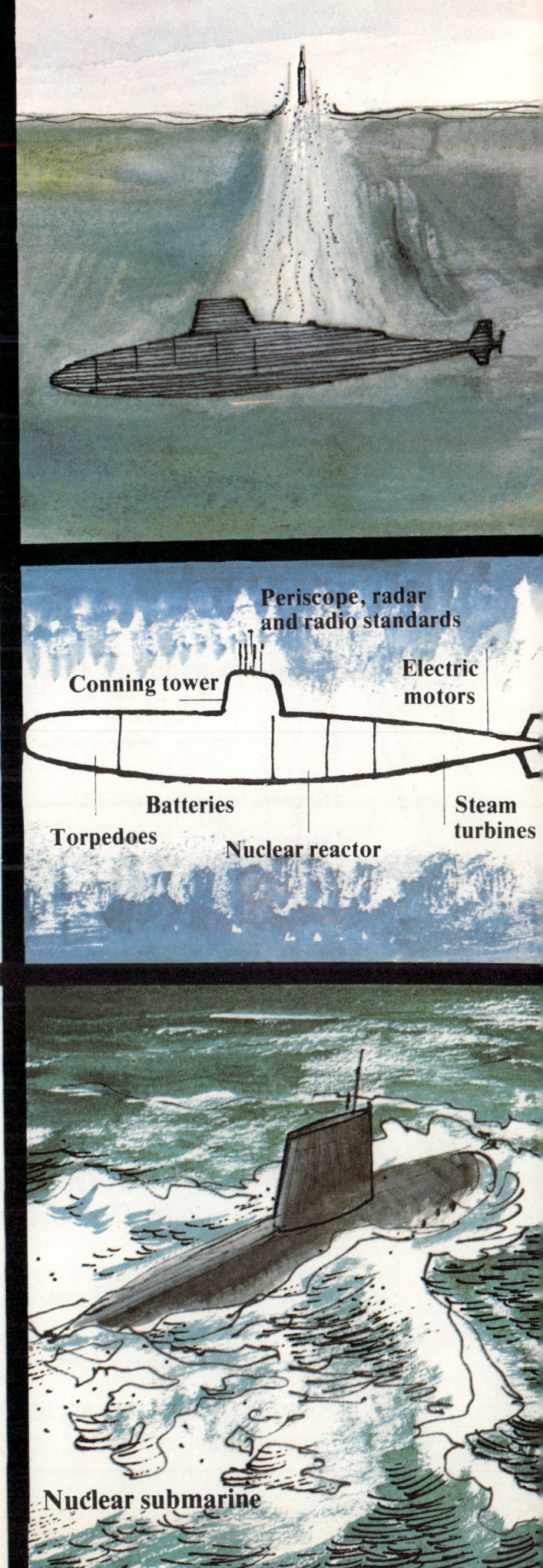

Motor powered submarines used electric power under water and diesel engines on and just beneath the surface. Electric batteries need no air to operate, but they have to be recharged and because they give off dangerous chlorine gas, the submarine has to risk surfacing to recharge its batteries.

Periscope, radar and radio standards

Conning tower

Electric motors

Batteries

Torpedoes

Nuclear reactor

Steam turbines

Modern submarines use nuclear power plants which work as well under water as above. These submarines can travel unlimited distances at high speed without refuelling.

With their special air conditioning and preserved foods, these submarines can disappear from sight and reappear in any part of the world.

The American **Nautilus** was the first nuclear submarine, launched in 1955.

Nuclear submarine

CARGOES—EXPORTS AND IMPORTS

One of the most important uses made of ships is to carry large loads, **cargoes**, of food and other goods between countries. Goods going out of a country are called **exports**. Goods coming into a country are called **imports**.

Some cargoes need special ships. Some cargoes are big and dry; some are big and wet; some are big and heavy; and some are easily broken.

There are also cargoes like butter, fish and meat that can start to go bad and smelly in heat or if they are not delivered quickly.

Refrigerator ship

Oil tanker

The ship in the top illustration is a **refrigerator** ship.

Refrigerator ships carry meat, fruit, fish and dairy products. They carry nothing else as their holds are small and the insulating material is easily damaged.

SHIPS FOR SPECIAL JOBS

Special ships have been built to do particular jobs.

Refrigerator ships are used to keep perishable cargoes cold and fresh. Before there were refrigerator ships these cargoes could only travel short distances, and some foods, such as fruit, were dried before shipping.

Huge **tankers** carry liquids like petrol and oil.

The ship in the bottom illustration is an **oil tanker**.

An oil tanker's cargo space is divided into a number of small tanks so that different grades of oil can be carried, and to stop the oil slopping about dangerously.

There are vessels specially made for the fishing industry. There are **trawlers** to catch the fish and **factory ships** to take the fish caught by the trawlers. Fish are also caught by surface nets from **drifters**, or by long lines from small **dories** which are carried by the mother ship.

Trawler

Phillipine canning factory ship

On the factory ships the fish are cleaned and frozen and packed ready to be carried to warehouses the moment the ship gets home again.

This saves a lot of time because everything is done at sea instead of waiting until the ship returns home.

Then there are ships that carry trains and motor cars.

Car ferry

Container ship

There are **container ships**. These carry big box containers, all neatly stacked aboard and easily brought to and carried from the ship by road or rail.

There are ships made for drilling for oil, like the one in the picture. There are ships that watch the weather and send reports of the weather changes.

Oil prospector ship

Ice-breaker

In Arctic waters **icebreakers** are needed to keep the shipping "roads" or **lanes** free.

Icebreakers have two propellers at each end of the hull to push through the ice.

21

PASSENGER SHIPS

Passenger ships have places to sit and eat, and comfortable cabins to sleep in. Some passenger ships are **liners**. These are owned by a company trading regularly only to selected ports. There are cargo liners too.

Passenger ship

Games deck

Big passenger liners have everything from games areas to shops and theatres on board. They include every luxury and are like floating hotels.

Luxury cruiser

Some people take a luxury cruise on a passenger liner rather than a holiday in a hotel on land.

Ferry boat

River boat

Little boats can carry passengers too, from the small **river boat** to the **ferry boat** that makes the journey across short stretches of water.

Hovercrafts are widely used to carry cars and people very quickly across short strips of water.

Hovercraft

DOCKS

Ships are loaded and unloaded with goods and passengers at the **docks**.

Docks have cranes and grabs to get the goods from the shore to the boats and from the boats to the shore.

Here in a port's docks ships are loaded and unloaded.

Ship escorted by tugs

Quay

Tug

Watertight gates

Cranes

They have buildings for the passengers to be checked, like the goods, before they are allowed into the country. Each country has its own laws about what or who shall be allowed in and out of their country. These laws are enforced by **customs** and **immigration officers**. Everything passing in or out of a country must go through customs or immigration. Each person must have a **passport**.

Storage warehouses

Warehouses

Customs

Dock

Tugs ready to assist the ship to open sea

Watertight gates

Warehouses

HARBOURS

To unload their cargoes, ships first come into **harbour**, a calm area of water often protected by walls from the open sea.

When large ships want to move into the quiet, protected waters of the harbour or when they want to leave the harbour to head for the open sea, they need help to move in the narrow places between other ships and their berths. A **berth** is the name for the place where a ship is tied up in the docks.

To help them there are little **tugboats** that, tied by ropes to the large ships, can pull them and move them slowly and safely to where they must go.

Large ships need tugboats to help them manoeuvre in narrow spaces and channels.

The ship may have to drop anchor while waiting for permission to enter the harbour.

Once in harbour the ship ties up to the dock.

Tugboat

Wreck buoy

NAVIGATING

At sea, the **port** side is the left hand side, and the **starboard** side is the right hand side.

To help ships move around each other and past buoys at night, they show different coloured lights. A **red** light for port and **green** for starboard.

Once out on the seas a ship must be kept safe from other ships and obstacles by following the international regulations for the prevention of collisions at sea. It is impossible to mark channels by walls or fences, but they can be shown on a map or chart.

Near the coast these channels are marked on the sea by floating markers called **buoys**. They are different shapes and colours to show which side of them a ship must pass. At night they have lights, and they have bells and whistles to be heard in the dark and fog. There are buoys for marking danger areas like wrecks and rocks too.

A ship turning to starboard gives one short blast on its whistle. If turning to port it gives two short blasts.

Can

Light

Channel

Buoy

CANALS

Some journeys can be made quicker and safer by making them shorter. So **canals** have been cut across land to let ships pass through to waters that could only have been reached before by a long voyage around a great mass of land.

Canal

Now **radar** is used in ships. It sends out radio signals that return an **echo** if they hit anything solid. These echoes are shown on a **radar screen** in the ship, which looks something like a television screen. The screen gives a diagram of the unseen dangers around the ship.

DANGERS AT SEA

Ships must sail safely without hitting rocks or other ships, even when it is night, or foggy, or in a storm.

Years ago, sailors had only their eyes to keep look-out for danger.

Echo soundi

MORE DANGERS AT SEA

Ships must be kept away from places where there are reefs and rocks, shallow waters or fierce currents. There must be warnings to keep the ships away. There must be bells and foghorns to be heard, and powerful, penetrating lights when it is dark.

To carry these warnings, **lighthouses** have been built, and **lightships** have been anchored where lighthouses cannot be built. Often men live in them to keep the lights working. They live there for long periods in all kinds of weather.

Lighthouse

**Air-sea rescue
helicopter**

The **air-sea
rescue** service
uses
helicopters
which can
hover low over
the sea and lift
distressed
people to
safety in a
harness.

RESCUE

The ship keeps in touch with land by **radio**. It has
foghorns to let other ships know it is there. If there is a
disaster, the ship has **lifeboats** to save the people on
board, and **lifebelts** to keep people afloat if they fall
into the water.

Sometimes, when all the safety devices fail to stop a
shipwreck, rescue services are called out. The
coastguard service, **air-sea rescue** service and the
lifeboat service have all saved the lives of many sailors
and passengers.

Helicopters
cannot be
flown in very
stormy
conditions, but
the brave
people who
man the
lifeboat service
will go out in
terrible
weather to
rescue
shipwrecked
people.

FUTURE TRAVEL BY SEA

Inventions change the ways in which we travel over the water for pleasure or for trade. New types of cargo or sources of power may bring new designs and different forms of travel.

Maybe one day, if fuel supplies run out, sailing ships will return again. Perhaps you have some ideas for what the future might bring?

Hoverchair

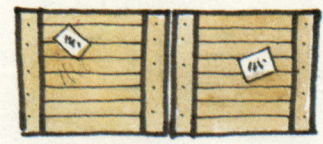

INDEX

	Page
Boat building	**4**
Canals	**28**
Cargo ships	**18–21**
Clippers	**11**
Dangers at sea	**28–29**
Docks	**24**
Early boats	**2**
Fishing ships	**20**
Future travel by sea	**31**
Harbours	**26**
Hovercraft	**15, 23**
Icebreaker	**21**
Navigating	**27**
Oars and paddles	**3**
Oil prospecting ship	**21**
Paddle steamers	**13**
Passenger ships	**20, 22–23**
Propeller	**14**
Rafts	**1**
Refrigerator ships	**19**
Rescue	**30**
Sailing ships	**6–11**
Steering	**8**
Submarines	**16–17**
Tankers	**19**
Trading and exploring	**5, 8**